THEME MUSIC

Arranged by Chad Johnson

ISBN 978-1-4768-2303-4

HAL•LEONARD®
CORPORATION
7777 W. BLUEMOUND RD. P.O. BOX 13819 MILWAUKEE, WI 53213

Visit Hal Leonard Online at
www.halleonard.com

Batman Theme

Words and Music by Neal Hefti

B

D.S. al Coda
(no repeat)

✦ **Coda**

Theme from E.T.
(The Extra-Terrestrial)
from the Universal Picture E.T. (THE EXTRA-TERRESTRIAL)

Music by John Williams

D

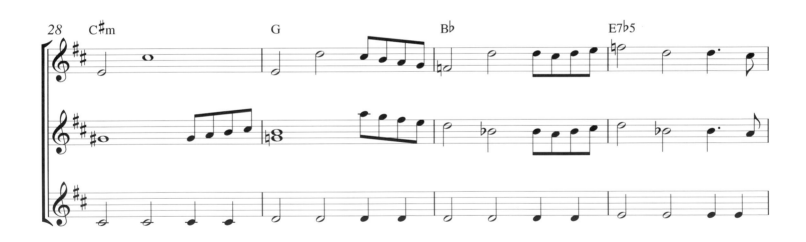

Forrest Gump – Main Title

(Feather Theme)

from the Paramount Motion Picture FORREST GUMP

Music by Alan Silvestri

B

The Godfather
(Love Theme)
from the Paramount Picture THE GODFATHER
By Nino Rota

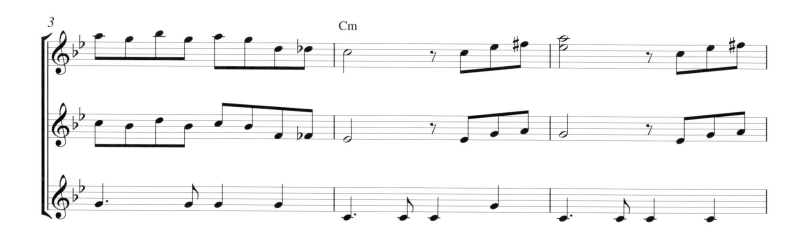

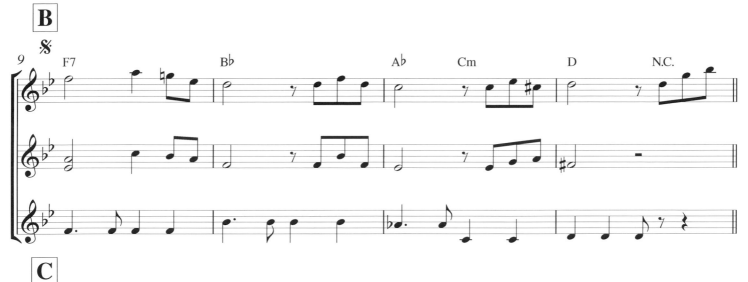

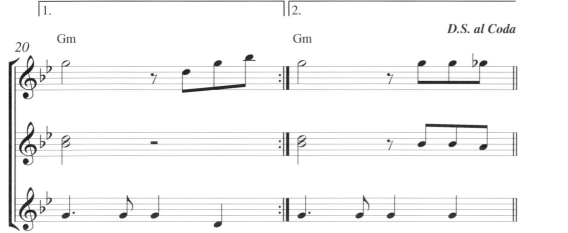

Hawaii Five-O Theme

from the Television Series

By Mort Stevens

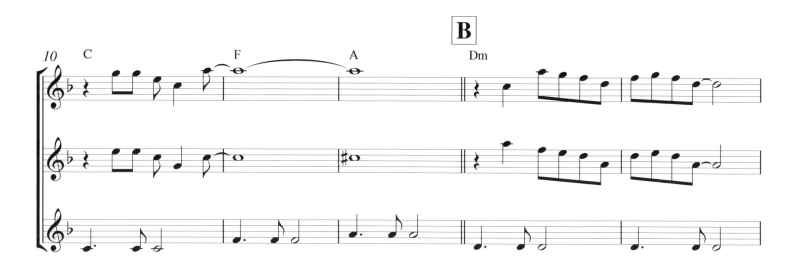

He's a Pirate

from Walt Disney Pictures' PIRATES OF THE CARIBBEAN: THE CURSE OF THE BLACK PEARL

Music by Klaus Badelt

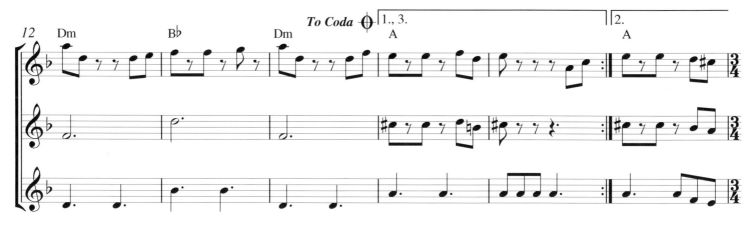

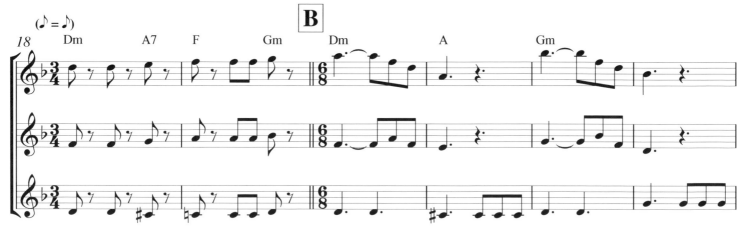

C

D.S. al Coda
(with repeat)

Coda

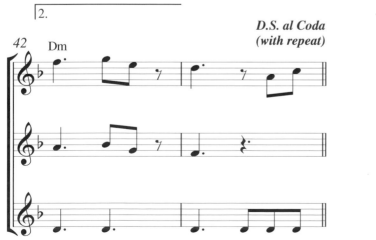

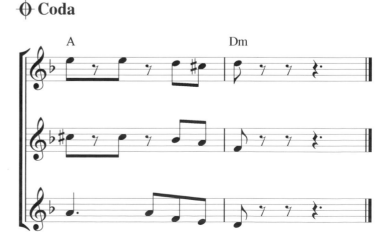

Linus and Lucy

By Vince Guaraldi

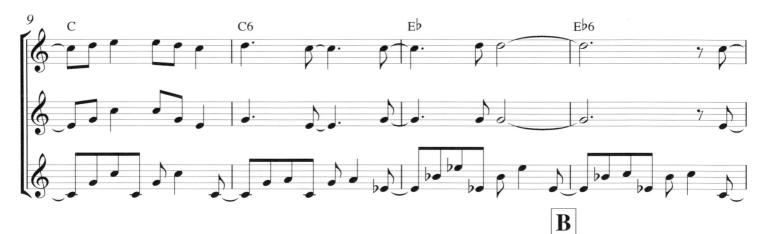

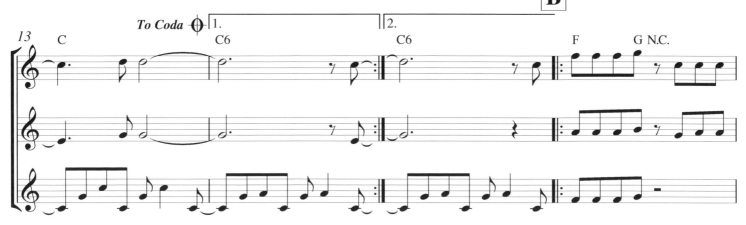

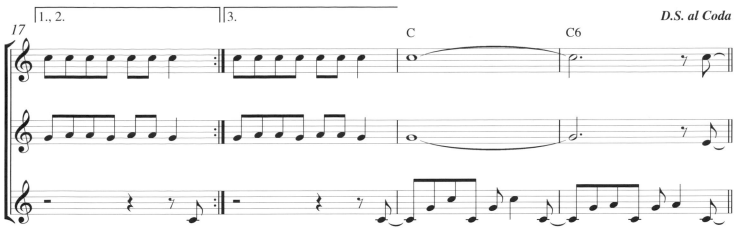

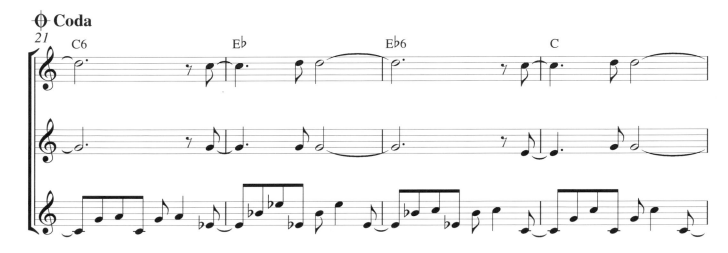

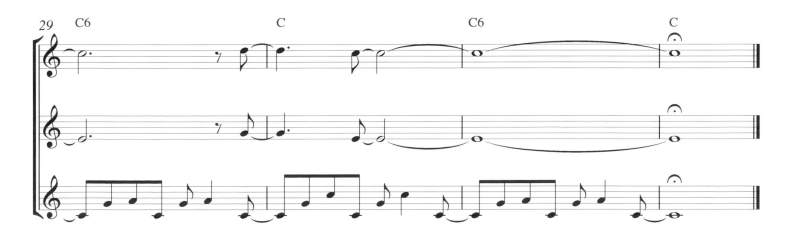

Mission: Impossible Theme

from the Paramount Television Series MISSION: IMPOSSIBLE
from the Paramount Motion Picture MISSION: IMPOSSIBLE

By Lalo Schifrin

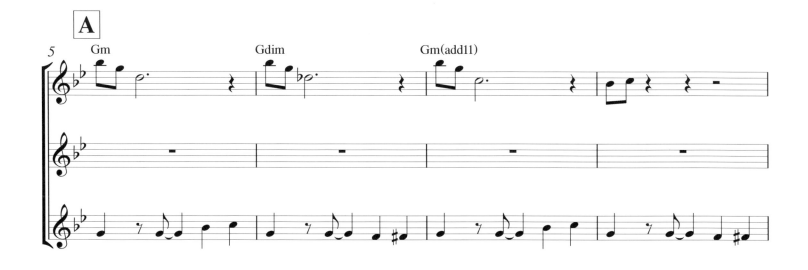

B

To Coda ⊕

D.C. al Coda

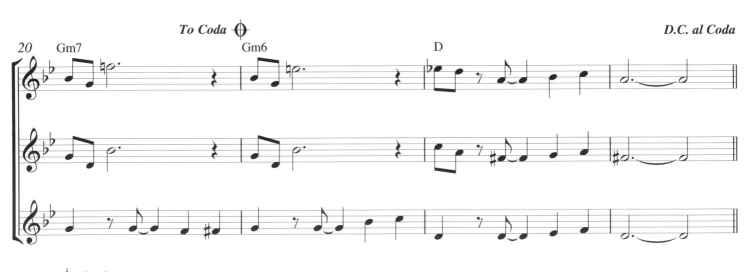

⊕ **Coda**

Peter Gunn

Theme Song from the Television Series

By Henry Mancini

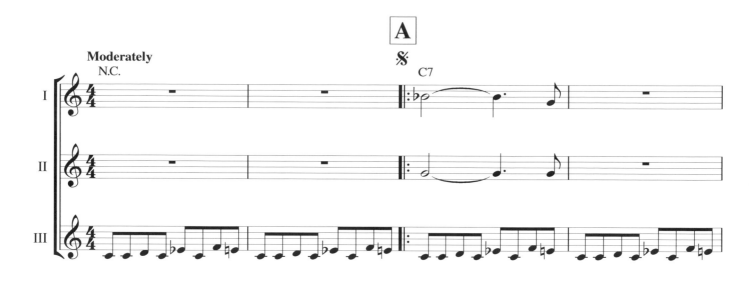

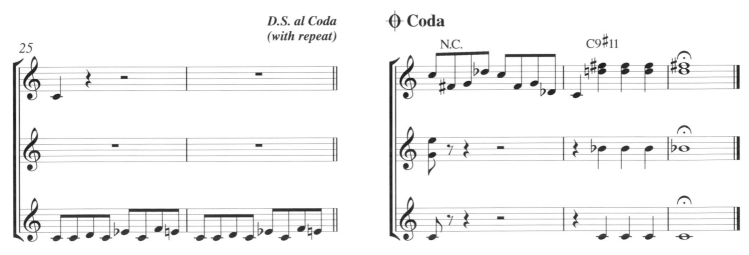

The Pink Panther

from THE PINK PANTHER

By Henry Mancini

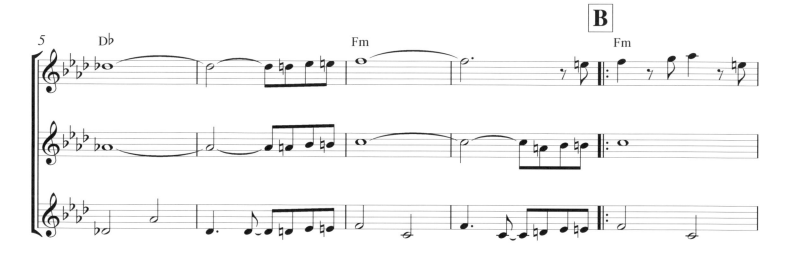

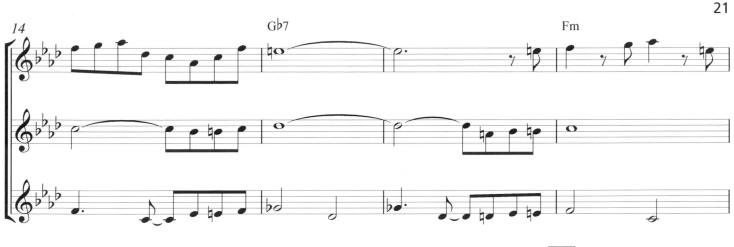

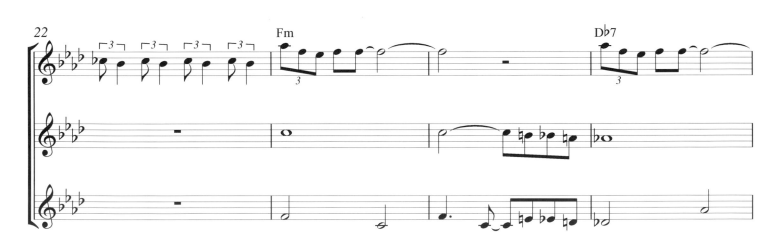

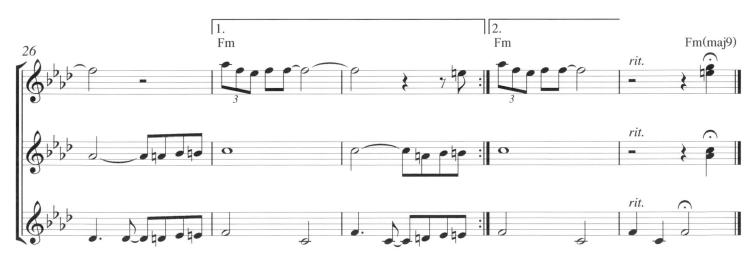

Raiders March

from the Paramount Motion Picture RAIDERS OF THE LOST ARK

Music by John Williams

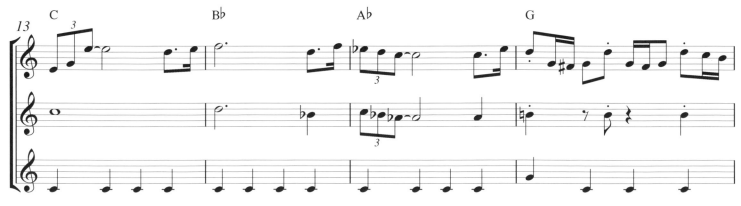

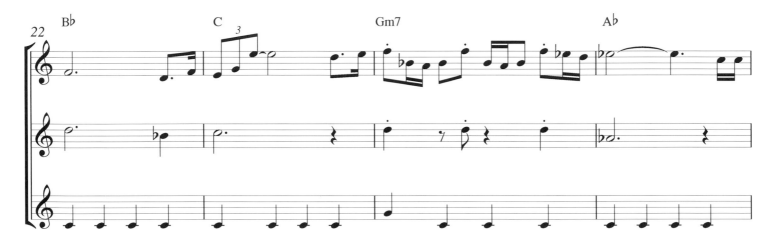

(Ghost)
Riders in the Sky
(A Cowboy Legend)

from RIDERS IN THE SKY

By Stan Jones

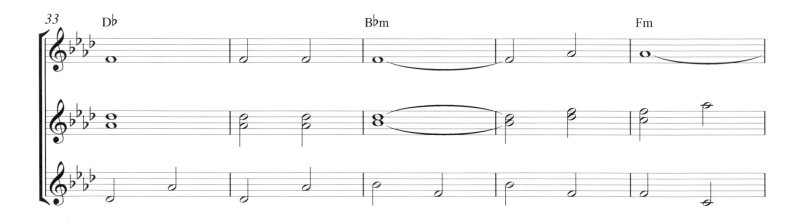

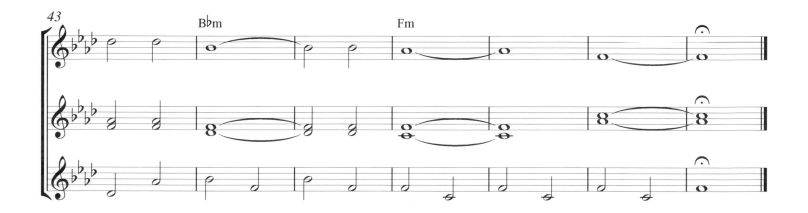

Theme from Spider Man

Written by Bob Harris and Paul Francis Webster

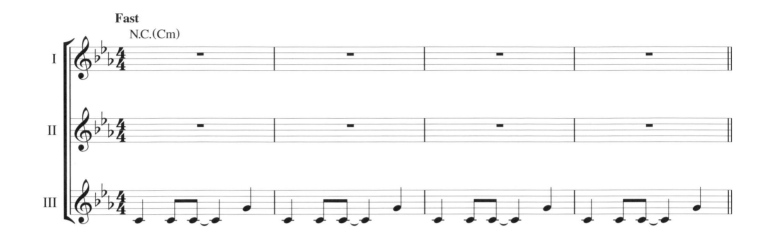

Theme from "Star Trek®"

from the Paramount Television Series STAR TREK

Words by Gene Roddenberry
Music by Alexander Courage

Coda

D.S. al Coda

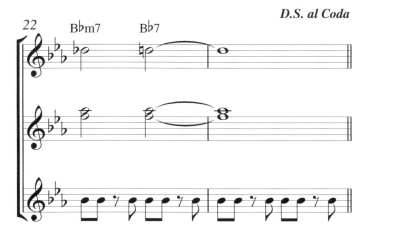

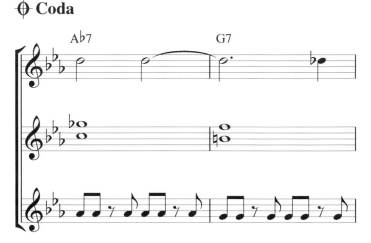

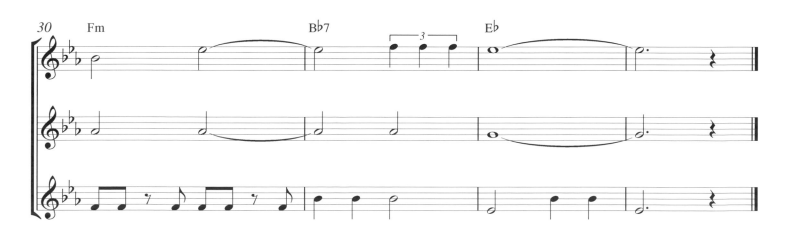

Theme from "Superman"

from SUPERMAN

Music by John Williams

NOTES FROM THE ARRANGER

Arranging for three ukuleles can be challenging because of the instrument's limited range. In standard tuning (G-C-E-A), there is only one octave plus a major sixth between the open C string and fret 12 on the A string. Certain melodies easily span this distance and more, so compromises sometimes had to be made.

Not all ukuleles have the same number of frets. If your uke has fewer than 15 frets, you may need to play certain phrases an octave lower (especially in Part I). Some phrases have already been transposed up or down an octave—this was only done out of necessity and kept to a minimum. A few songs require every inch of available fretboard, but fret 15 on the first string (high C) is the limit, and this is extremely rare.

The three voices will sometimes cross as a result of range limitations. If Part III is considered to be the "bass" line, keep in mind that the lowest available "bass" notes are sometimes on the first string! However, if you own a baritone ukulele, almost all of the notes in Part III could be played an octave lower (except the open C string and C♯ on fret 1), thus providing a more effective bass line.

Despite the above caveats, I believe that the spirit of these songs has been preserved, and I hope you enjoy playing these arrangements as much as I enjoyed creating them. By the way, a fourth ensemble part can be added by strumming along with the chord symbols!

– Chad Johnson

SOPRANO, CONCERT & TENOR FRETBOARD

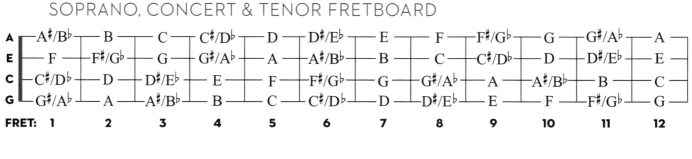

BARITONE FRETBOARD

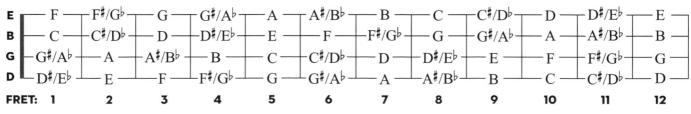